Steam Memories on Shed: 1950's – 1

No. 109: Scottish Region ENGINE SHEDS
66B to 68D & their Motive Power

Copyright Book Law Publications 2019
ISBN 978-1-909625-04-1

INTRODUCTION

This album highlights eleven steam motive power depots which were all in the territory covered by the former London Midland & Scottish Railway who in turn inherited those depots from the Caledonian Railway and the Glasgow & South Western Railway. It will be noted that the sheds of the latter company presented mainly something of a building standard design – the Galloway shed – which was generally stone built with arched openings and arched windows, along with lofty pitched roofs. Other ex-G&SW sheds were of a later design which we will review as we go along. The Caledonian didn't really present a standard format except perhaps in roof types, with transverse roofs taking over from earlier pitched roofs.

The motive power residing at these engine sheds mainly consisted of mixed traffic, goods, or shunting engines because these particular establishments were involved in moving the freight traffic around the region, as well as providing the motive power for local and secondary passenger services. One thing we can rely on is the mix of motive power with pre-Grouping classes rubbing shoulders with the LMS and British Railways standard types.

We would like to thank the good offices of the Armstrong Railway Photographic Trust (ARPT) for their continued support of this series. Also, some individual photographers have supplied material for which we are very grateful as it adds to our eclectic mixture of images. Thank you all.

David Dunn, Cramlington, January 2019.

(Cover)   **See page 11**

(Title page)   **More than four-year old BR Standard Cl.4 No.80030 of Corkerhill looks rather smart for the period outside Ayr shed on 19th May 1956.** *F.W. Hampson.*

Printed and bound by The Amadeus Press, Cleckheaton, West Yorkshire
First published in the United Kingdom by Book Law Publications, 382 Carlton Hill, Nottingham, NG4 1JA

66B MOTHERWELL

The south end of Motherwell shed yard on 24th September 1961. The locomotive stud is overwhelmingly made up of ex-LMS Standard classes; keeping them company are a couple of WD Austerity 2-10-0s, and a single ex-Caley 2F. The allocation at this shed certainly altered drastically during the seventeen years from Nationalisation to 66B's closure to steam in 1967. On 31st December 1947 some 137 locomotives called Motherwell home; these consisted two LMS Cl.3 2-6-2T; two LMS 4F 0-6-0; eighteen Stanier Cl.5; seven Stanier 8F; eight ex-CR 3P 4-4-0; eighteen ex-CR 4MT 4-6-0; four ex-CR 2P 0-4-4T; three ex-CR 0-4-0ST; one ex-CR 2F 0-6-0T; twenty-two ex-CR 3F 0-6-0T; forty-one ex-CR 2F 0-6-0; eleven ex-CR 3F 0-6-0. Two years later the numbers were down to a 116 total including seven WD 2-8-0s along with twelve WD 2-10-0s which had replaced some of the older ex-Caley 0-6-0s along with the Stanier 8Fs which had migrated south to the London Midland Region. Ten years later the numbers had changed yet again with the total standing at 89 steam locomotives with BR Standards taking the place of former Caledonian types which now numbered just thirty-nine, new 350 h.p. 0-6-0 diesel-electric shunting locomotives had gradually infiltrated since December 1955 so that by the summer of 1958 some nineteen of them were resident with four 204 h.p. 0-4-0 diesel-mechanical joining them in December 1959. As one of the last bastions of steam in Scotland, the end at Motherwell came in May 1967 and the final seven locomotive were taken away for scrap. 66B was now a fully-fledged diesel depot without an allocation but providing stabling room for dozens of the Scottish Regions best – and worst – performing locomotives but that's another story. The re-roofing of 1955 – see later – is very evident as are the new gables constructed from lightweight cladding which replaced the original stone above the entrances. *Christopher Campbell.*

A sign of the times – Stanier Cl.5 No.44923 awaiting its next job at Motherwell on Saturday 16th May 1964; in actuality the engine was just weeks away from withdrawal! Having initially been allocated new to Blackpool in January 1946, this Crewe-built 4-6-0 was transferred with sister No.4922 to St Rollox Balornock shed in February 1946. It was there she remained until withdrawn in June 1964. Note the different levels of the yard at this point; it must have been too easy to bury the nearest track with ash, clinker and firebox debris during busy periods. Considering Motherwell's allocation consisted well in excess of a hundred and ten locomotives, there was very little investment in the depot's facilities by either the LMS or British Railways. The coaling remained pivoted around two ancient timber framed, single-faced coaling stages – one at each end of the shed yard – where Herculean feats were carried out by the coalmen to keep those tenders and bunkers full. The ash disposal facility was as seen here already with wheel barrows, shovels, sweat, and grime coming together to shift what must have been a hundred tons or more of firebox and smokebox waste every week. No mechanical aids here right to the end of steam. Motherwell was a so-called Main shed under the former LMS scheme but it did not necessarily attract the same monetary funds as most of the other Main depots with much smaller allocations – Corkerhill, Inverness, Perth, and indeed some of the lesser Garage sheds located in England. However, during the early era of diesel power the depot remained open for business and though virtually unaltered from its life under steam, it managed to become the main diesel servicing depot in Scotland with purpose-built depots being discarded and demolished. *A. Ives (ARPT).*

(*opposite, top*) A visitor from Dundee prepares to return home on 22nd May 1949! Thompson B1 No.61101 rides the 70ft diameter turntable which had but one entrance/exit line and was located in the south-west corner of the depot yard. Provided as early as 1906, the turntable had been fitted with a vacuum tractor by the LMS – one of the few examples of investment here – in the 1930s. However, the appliance had been affected from its initial installation by subsidence in this heavily mined area of the country. Indeed, it may well have been the reason why monolithic coaling plants and ash plants were never provided here for fear of collapse due to coal mining. It was, apparently, only necessary for mine owners to advise landowners of the approach of mine workings and in the case of the railways it was necessary only where passenger lines were concerned; they could only dig to within 40-foot of an imaginary vertical line from the boundary of the railway. Goods lines and their likes' and facilities such as engine sheds could, by law, be undermined! *K.H. Cockerill (ARPT).*

This rather nice bogie coach was part of the Motherwell Breakdown train on 1st April 1961 and was classified as a Riding Van, allocated to Motherwell and given the number DE320402. That is all we know about it, oh and the fact that it still had curtains hanging in the saloon. It looks as though it once had corridor connections but these have been literally boarded-up for the vehicles' final role in its history. The mountain forming the background on the east side of the depot consisted of locally produced industrial waste. Note that the stone gables at this end of the shed have been largely untouched except for a small portion on each apex where the 1955 roof refurbishment was secured with new brickwork. *N.W. Skinner (ARPT).*

The north end of the shed with Kingmoor based BR 9F No.92021 polluting the yard on an unknown date between June 1964, when it transferred to Kingmoor from Kettering, and July 1965 when it was moved to Birkenhead. This was of course one of the former Crosti-boiler equipped members of the class which was converted to a conventional boiler in June 1960 after the Crosti 'experience' was initially abandoned in September 1959 when classmate No.92026 was converted. The batch of Crosti-fitted engines – 92020-92029 – had all be dealt with by June 1962 but prior to the conversions a number of modifications were made to the 'Crosti ten' in order to get out of them what had been proposed by the design. The first mod was the fitting of a smoke deflector over the side chimney; next the preheaters were re-tubed on all ten between September 1956 and May 1957 which was followed by the fitting of new blast chambers and chimneys during the eight months March to October 1957. This final mod was carried out on some engines at the same time as re-tubing the preheater. Storage pending the removal of the Crosti section of the boiler (the preheater beneath the larger upper boiler) started in April 1959 and in one case lasted until March 1962 but eventually all ten were converted to conventional steaming, the last being No.92022 in June 1962. Study of the recorded mileage's of the ten Crosti engines during the years 1955 to 1959 reveal that the group were certainly under-performing compared to the other Standard 9Fs. During their first full year of operation only three of them recorded more than 23,000 miles whilst the others were struggling to better 21,000 miles. It didn't get much better the following years with highs of 24,100 and lows of 17,900! 1959 saw mileage's ranging from zero to 21,800 although the latter figure was somewhat extreme and actual the average was less than 6,000 miles. Even the WD Austerity 2-8-0s were bettering 25,000 miles on average! *Kevin Hudspith.*

When British Railways came into being, Motherwell shed had eighteen – the whole class – of these former Caledonian and early LMS Class 4P 4-6-0s on its books including this example No.54640 which was photographed at Motherwell on 1st October 1950. At Grouping the LMS had inherited six of these tender engines – Nos.14650 to 14655 (Caley Class 60) – and then during 1925 and 1926 they built another twenty of a similar design – Nos.14630 to 14649 – at St Rollox; these had slightly larger cylinders with half an inch added to the diameter and weighted a little less too. Some twenty-five years earlier the Caledonian had beforehand passed on to the LMS some thirty-seven 4-6-0s which did not survive to Nationalisation: '55' Cl. 4P Nos.14600 to 14608 gone by end of 1937; '908' Cl. 4P Nos.14609 to 14618 gone by end of 1935; '191' Cl. 4P Nos.14619 to 14626 gone by end of 1945; '903' or 'Cardean' Cl. 4P Nos.14752 to 14755 gone by end of 1930 (No.907 which would have been 14756 was scrapped after being involved in the terrible crash at Quintinshill in 1915); '49' Cl. 4P Nos.14740 and 14751 gone in 1933; '956' Cl. 5P Nos.14800 to 14803 gone by end of 1935. Of course the LMS also inherited a myriad of 4-6-0 tender engines from both the Glasgow & South Western, and the Highland. Our subject locomotive was in fact amongst the three withdrawn in 1952, the penultimate year of the class. *K.H. Cockerill (ARPT).*

During the period when the shed roof was renewed, BR Standard Cl.4 No.76000 stables beneath the myriad of lightweight tie-bars, cross-bars and assorted roof supports on Sunday 29th May 1955. Just above the cab roof of the 2-6-0 can be seen the 30-ton hoist which was located on No.8 road and supplemented an earlier 30-ton hoist provided in the two-road repair shop accessed at the north-west end of the shed. No.76000 had arrived at 66B new from Horwich in December 1952 and was quickly followed by sisters 76001 to 76004. Three of them, including our subject engine remained loyal to Motherwell shed throughout their lives until withdrawal. No.76000 was the last of them being condemned in May 1967. No.76002 and 76003 were withdrawn in January 1967 and December 1966 respectively. Other Cl.4s were allocated new to 66B but they too moved on to other depots. *F.W. Hampson (ARPT).*

A further roof reconstruction view on that Sunday in May 1955 but this from the north yard with resident 2F No.57328 attached to a tender full of 'mixed quality' coal! The aforementioned gable apex brick replacement scheme is seen in the making with the actual bricks themselves dumped on the ground. *F.W. Hampson (ARPT)*.

Staying in the north yard, we go back in time to the latter months of 1954 when the first vestiges of roof reconstruction was taking place over the two western-most roads of the running shed. Resident 3P No.54465 is stabled alongside the main line to Coatbridge – over which the photographer has just crossed to get the right angle on the locomotive! Sister No.54453, another Motherwell engine butts into the frame. *K.H. Cockerill (ARPT).*

(*opposite, top*) Some might title this image as 'A rose between two thorns!' but beauty alone does not a locomotive make? A rather smart resident 3P No.54460 is flanked by a pair of the WD 'Austerities' which called Motherwell home. Although undated, this image must have been recorded pre-winter 1954 when roof repairs were started. (*opposite*) Accident damage on this scale could be described as superficial but quite a bit of 2F No.57433 would have to be replaced before the 0-6-0 re-entered service. The where and when of the incident is unrecorded. *Both K.H. Cockerill (ARPT).*

How fortunes changed! 3P No.54465 heads a line of condemned locomotives at the north end of the siding skirting the main line to Coatbridge on 1ˢᵗ April 1961. Except for the missing wheelset, the 4-4-0 is complete in every respect but the odds are against it returning to service and it was eventually withdrawn in October of the following year and sold to the local scrap giant at Wishaw. For the record, No.54460 which we saw earlier was condemned in October 1955. Note the new diesel shunters looking on from the shed yard *N.W. Skinner (ARPT).*

The morning sun highlights Kingmoor's Stanier 8F No.48612 stabled at the north end of the shed on 3rd April 1961. The 2-8-0 has taken a knock recently but that bent running plate would not be straightened out until the next works visit at Horwich some twelve-months hence. Before the WD 2-8-0 and 2-10-0s arrived here, Motherwell acquired a batch of twenty-two of these superb engines for working its long distance freight trains during WWII and thereafter. Starting in April 1942 the acquisitions went as follows – 8183 to 8188; October 1942 and into February 1943 – 8152 to 8160; July 1943 – 8024, 8069, 8078, 8079, 8085; and finally 8321 and 8341 in February 1944. A few moved on to other places fairly quickly but the majority remained into June 1946 when four departed, and the final months of the LMS and then into the BR period, the last three to go being Nos.48184 to 48186 in September 1948. *N.W. Skinner (ARPT).*

13

This rather interesting view at the south end of Motherwell depot yard on 3rd April 1961 shows from the left: (1) the rear of the south end manual coaling stage which by some miracle of nature and man combined, remained standing and operational until the end of steam in 1967. The stonework is in fact leaning but has been halted in its endeavours to collapse by strengthening bars and old rail carefully woven through the fabric of the building to prevent catastrophe. (2) 3F 0-6-0T No.56337 was yet another long-time resident of 66B and was now becoming a liability with a split chimney and distorted smokebox. Withdrawal was in fact just weeks away during July. The tank came to Motherwell from Polmadie after WWII and spent the rest of its life at the shed. By Nationalisation some twenty or so of its kind were allocated here for much of the early 1950s but the loss of shunting jobs to the new diesel classes saw their numbers drop some two-thirds by 1960. (3) the end of the coaling stage ramp with carefully stacked timbers holding up the rails which carried the loaded wagons and the gangway. This structure replaced the original stone and brick construction which was badly affected by subsidence throughout the life of the stage. (4) the Muir Street bridge had seen some strengthening applied during its lifetime! (5) The spur to the turntable out of frame on the right. Note the authorisation signal which controlled the exit from the turntable and was equipped with a telephone for communication to the signal box beyond the bridge and which controlled the shed entrance/exit lines. *N.W. Skinner (ARPT).*

Resident WD Austerity 2-10-0 No.90761 stabled at the north end of the running shed on 9th June 1962. This class of locomotive was associated with Motherwell throughout their lives and our subject here was allocated to 66B on 23rd March 1949 as WD No.73785 (renumbered in May 1949) and remained working from the depot until withdrawn on 29th November 1962. Without going into the life history of the class it is worth noting that fourteen of the twenty-five members actually finished their BR careers at Motherwell, most of them having been loyal to the shed since BR purchased them in the late '40s thus: 90750 – 8th October 1949 to l 9th May 1962 withdrawal; 90751 – 7th October 1961 to 29th December 1962 withdrawal; 90752 – 8th October 1949 to 19th December 1961 withdrawal; 90754 – 25th May 1950 to 6th July 1961 withdrawal; 90756 – 17th June 1950 to 29th December 1962 withdrawal; 90758 – 16th June 1950 to 29th December 1962 withdrawal; 90760 – 26th March 1949 to 9th May 1962 withdrawal; 90761 – 23rd April 1949 to 29th November 1962 withdrawal; 90762 – 16th February 1949 to 29th December 1962 withdrawal; 90764 – 12th September 1959 to 17th December 1962 withdrawal; 90767 – 7th October 1961 to 29th December 1962 withdrawal; 90770 – 19th March 1949 to 29th December 1962 withdrawal; 90771 – 12th September 1959 to 29th December 1962 withdrawal; 90772 – 29th October 1962 to 29th December 1962 withdrawal. Of that batch five went to Cowlairs for breaking up and nine were sent to Darlington for scrapping; our subject engine went to the latter venue for the last rites which were performed during the week ending Saturday 16th November 1963! Note the coal stage at the north end of the yard which was as ramshackle and dilapidated as its counterpart at the south end. *C.J.B. Sanderson (ARPT).*

Said coal stage on 29th April 1963 when it was abandoned. By now its coaling road was just another length of track to store redundant and withdrawn locomotives as witness one-buffer No.57384 and WD 2-10-0 No.90771. For anyone modelling this piece of Caledonian history, the image is revealing plenty of detail on and within the stage including those internal brackets fixing the roof to the walls and fashioned from redundant running rail; who said BR wasted money? Or did the LMS fit those brackets? *C.J.B. Sanderson (ARPT).*

The footbridge which connected the engine shed with the outside world and which today would have been approved by the H&SE as the only way to get into the shed from the main pedestrian entrance. However, within two minutes of blessing the footbridge, the H&SE would then have condemned the structure as being unsafe and therefore rendering the pedestrian entrance to Motherwell engine shed well and truly sealed-off until a new facility had been provided! Beneath the bridge on this 29th day of April 1963 are further examples of abandoned steam with 2F No.57370 with a spring missing from the tender, and Cl.3 No.40186 which was condemned here at Motherwell its home shed in December 1962 but the eagle-eyed will note the 66C Hamilton shed plate being worn. Now, I know it's a long shot but that shed plate is somewhat disconcerting and to this compiler one explanation is that the recent severe winter saw many diesel locomotives and units failing throughout the country. Hamilton being something of a DMU depot would have been hard hit probably during those extremes of cold weather. The authorities saw no alternative but to resurrect withdrawn steam locomotives – we must remember that many steam locomotives at this time were written off simply because they were steam or had been replaced by diesels – which were still mechanically sound to haul passenger trains. The Cl.3s were ideal for the local suburban work and perhaps they had a week or so working those 'stoppers' again. Hamilton fixed their plate optimistically and never removed it. *C.J.B. Sanderson (ARPT).*

18 *(above & top)* **Self-explanatory! Vehicles in the Hamilton breakdown train 1950.** *C.J.B. Sanderson (ARPT).*

Hamilton's substantial coaling stage had two faces, each with two drops. The fact that the stage supported the depot's water supply tank ensured a structure built to last even in this mining subsidence affected area and so both stone and brick walls were provided, the thickness of the brick section being visible in two of the openings. Hamilton West engine shed to give the depot its full title was opened in 1884; it consisted a ten-road building constructed of timber much like the shed at Polmadie before rebuilding. A two-road repair shop with hoist was provided on the east side of the shed. Hamilton was never rebuilt but it was reduced in size when subsidence caused the demolition of the front – northern – section of the building across all ten roads during the LMS period. Dieselisation of the local passenger services and the steady closure of collieries in the BR period saw steam banished from the depot in November 1962 – just as that historical winter was brewing – so that the place could be used exclusively by DMUs. This image from 6th June 1953 shows ex-CR 4P 4-6-0 No.54639 being coaled during its final six months of existence. Hamilton was home to a pair of these handsome engines – Nos.54638 and 54639 – during the short time the engines worked in BR days. No.54638 had gone in May 1951! It might be remembered that Hamilton was home to the three LMS diesel railcars numbered 29950, 29951, and 29952. The early association appears to have ensured a longer life for the depot which was still operational some fifteen years after steam had vacated. *C.J.B. Sanderson (ARPT).*

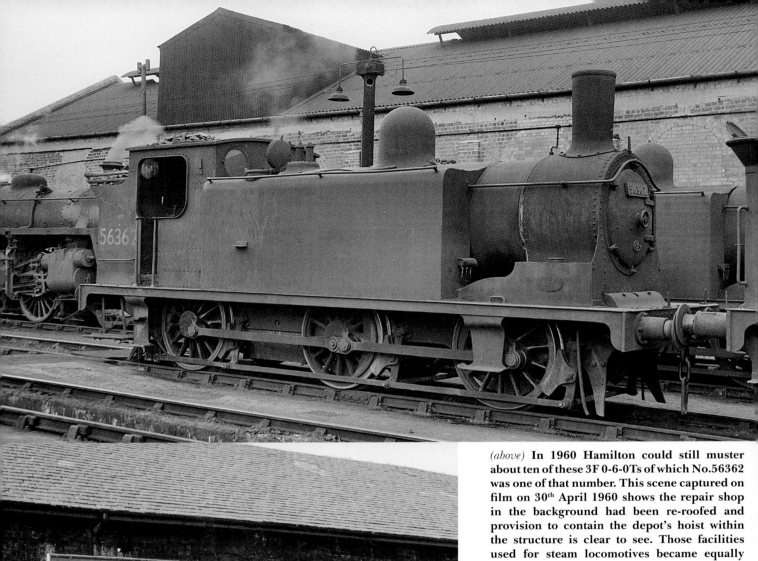

(above) **In 1960 Hamilton could still muster about ten of these 3F 0-6-0Ts of which No.56362 was one of that number. This scene captured on film on 30th April 1960 shows the repair shop in the background had been re-roofed and provision to contain the depot's hoist within the structure is clear to see. Those facilities used for steam locomotives became equally useful for the diesel railcars which replaced steam at 66C. After near twenty years working from Hamilton – it went there during WWII – No.56362 was withdrawn at the shed in August 1961 and sent to the BR works at Cowlairs for scrapping.** *C.J.B. Sanderson (ARPT).*

(left) **A nicely rendered wooden sign still located on the top of the amenities block at Hamilton on 5th April 1980 long after the shed had closed.** *B. Hildreth.*

66D GREENOCK (LADYBURN)

A regular sight at Ladyburn was a row or two of shunting tanks of various classes with fifteen or so resident throughout WWII. This is a line-up on 19th May 1956 with the following 0-6-0Ts in no particular order: 47167, 56157, 56163, 56173, and 56288. *F.W. Hampson (ARPT).*

(opposite) **'Pug' No.16031 at Greenock Ladyburn in 1950 with LMS tender No.341010. At this time Ladyburn had three of these 0-4-0STs: 56028, 56031, and 56035 to give them the allocated BR numbers. Ten years later the latter two of the trio were still resident at 66D. On 12th May 1951 No.16031 was observed coupled to Engine Tender M313248 at Ladyburn shed; obviously changing of these vehicles was a regular occurrence.** *C.J.B. Sanderson (ARPT).* *(opposite, bottom)* **The Fowler Cl.4 tanks resident in Scotland since their introduction in the winter of 1933 numbered ten engines, all with the enclosed cab, and No.42400 being amongst them. They were allocated to Ladyburn when this image was recorded on 12th May 1951. The ten then moved on, to English sheds in a straight swap for newer Fairburn Cl.4s in 1954, this particular 2-6-4T going to Stoke, the others to Bangor, Monument Lane, and Springs Branch, Wigan.** *C.J.B. Sanderson (ARPT).*

Ladyburn on 16th May 1964 with its modern but much reduced fleet of 2-6-4T fleet consisting no more than a dozen of these Fairburn Class 4s with some BR Standard Cl.4s supplementing the stud. These engines were amongst those imported from England in exchange for the ten Fowler models. The shed roof is now in its final form and built over five of the original eight roads. *A. Ives (ARPT).*

This former Great Northern six-wheel composite coach was resident at Ladyburn shed on 12th May 1951. Identified as CC 53 with LNER lettering, the vehicle was probably visiting in conjunction with the shed rebuilding and was part of the Civil Engineers fleet although we are open to suggestions and correction. It had a paint date of 7th June 1946 on its solebar and a plate on the end containing dimensional information but the paintwork was somewhat flaky and therefore unreadable. *C.J.B. Sanderson (ARPT).*

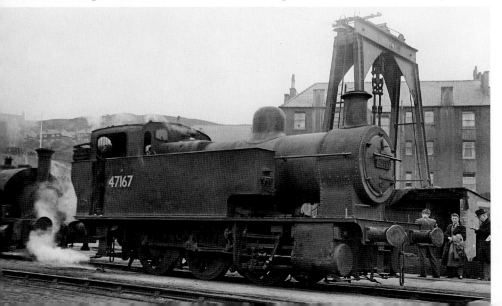

(left) **Whilst visiting enthusiasts take stock and compare notes, 2F No.47167 is stabled over an inspection pit alongside the depot's 40-ton hoist.** *C.J.B. Sanderson (ARPT).*

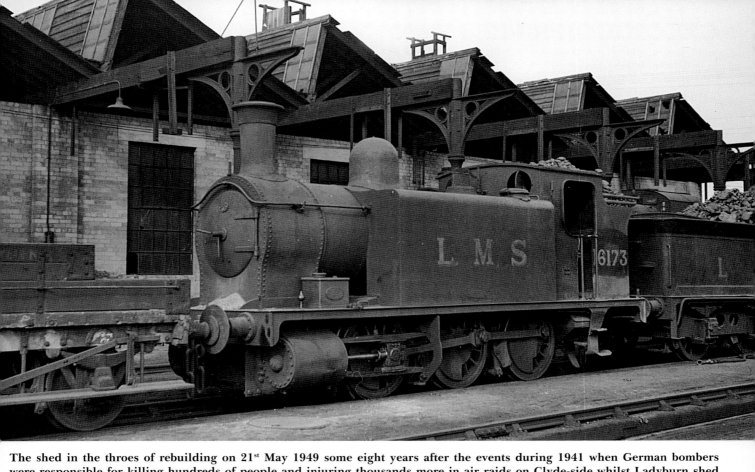

The shed in the throes of rebuilding on 21st May 1949 some eight years after the events during 1941 when German bombers were responsible for killing hundreds of people and injuring thousands more in air raids on Clyde-side whilst Ladyburn shed suffered bomb damage too and lost an engine in the shape of 4-4-0 No.14356. Here, resident engines stabled where they could. 'Beetlecrusher' No.16173 was still wearing its old company identification and was looking rather filthy although everything was during that transition period when BR came into being. The last of the twenty-three McIntosh 2F 0-6-0T built by the CR between 1911 and 1921, No.16173 carried Caledonian No.515 when put into traffic in 1921. All of the class survived to become BR property and have 40000 added to their numbers. The first withdrawal took place in 1958 and all were gone by the end of 1962. Ladyburn shed had four of the class allocated in 1934 and nearby Princes Pier had another; No.16173 was one of a pair living over at Dundee at that time. Both Dawsholm and Polmadie had five each whilst the others were spread around. WWII brought changes to the distribution of the class with the Greenock sheds having seven between them including 16173, Polmadie likewise with seven and Dawsholm six, two at Grangemouth and one at Balornock. Peacetime saw another slight re-distribution with Greenock and Polmadie reverting to six apiece again whilst Dawsholm – with its Yoker sub shed – increased its share to seven, Grangemouth kept two, St Rollox kept its singleton and Motherwell gained one. In BR days nothing changed radically but Corkerhill, Eastfield and Kipps all used them. The distribution of the class amongst the various scrapping venues was similar to the lifetime allocations with Inverurie taking care of seven – including 56173, Kilmarnock did six, Cowlairs and Heatheryknowe C&W one each; private yards took eight with Connels of Calder having five, Motherwell M&S two, and McLellan at Langloan just one. No.56173 was withdrawn in May 1961 from Greenock, one of nine ending their days at the shed. This view reveals the otherwise hidden detail of a northlight style roof and its supporting wood and ironwork. *K.H. Cockerill (ARPT).*

GREENOCK (PRINCES PIER)

'Dock Tank' No.7169 – wearing the old LMS 27B Greenock shedplate – trundles across the shed yard at Princes Pier on Saturday 21st May 1949 to get to a water column and the turntable. The depot's coaling stage – a slightly elevated wagon road with a substantial screen and sloping roofed cover and provided by the LMS in 1930 – stands defiantly to ward off any north-easterly winds which might delay the coaling process; the fact that whilst this part of Scotland gets most of its weather from the west and south does not appear to have been considered. Princes Pier was a sub shed of Greenock Ladyburn but the former G&SW shed was still being worked hard supplying engines for boat trains and shunting duties. The three-road engine shed dated from 1869 and remained in its original form until 1950 when re-roofing was necessary and the three width restricted arched doorways were eliminated in favour of a single span created by a steel girder. It appears that one of these 0-6-0 tank engines had always been allocated to this shed as witness the May 1935 listings where 7109 (formerly 11279 and later 7169) was resident. Of the ten strong class at that time five worked in Scotland 11272, 11273 at Dalry Road shed, and 11277 and 11278 at Ardrossan; the others were based in England. The Second World War brought Nos.11277 and 11278 – now renumbered 7167 and 7168 – to Greenock although to Ladyburn shed rather than Princes Pier and that situation remained unchanged until withdrawals started in September 1959 when our subject engine here was condemned, followed by No.47167 in July 1960; the last of the trio was No.47168 in October 1962. However, one of the Edinburgh survivors from Dalry Road – No.47162 had succumbed in December 1959 at St Margarets – was transferred to Ladyburn to be withdrawn in January 1963. *K.H. Cockerill (ARPT).*

Don't get the impression that this album is top heavy with rolling stock, it isn't but we are presenting some rather nice pieces of old passenger stock such as this former Midland Railway 6-wheeler which was latterly employed by the Motive Power Department at Stranraer but on 12th May 1951 was dumped on a siding at the western end of Greenock Princes Pier shed yard alongside the shed outlet. The number on the vehicle is rather faded but appears to be 96572 which we're sure some of you carriage fans out there will know immediately where the vehicle was built and when, and what happened to it after its foray on the Clyde. *C.J.B. Sanderson (ARPT).*

Besides the three roads under cover inside the engine shed at Princes Pier, there was another area in the depot yard west of the shed where four parallel sidings were laid down to accommodate locomotives. Only one of the sidings had a pit but it was nevertheless a useful place to stable engines awaiting duty or perhaps storing those taken out of service for whatever reason. On 12th May 1951 former LMS Compound No.41131 was stored after works attention. The 4P was one of Polmadie's allocated pair at this time – the other was No.40916 – which it had kept since Nationalisation, remnants of the time when Polmadie had a dozen of the class on the books in 1935 but that number was decreasing gradually so that by 1944 only seven were resident. Why 66A kept hold of the pair of Compounds is unknown; events such as this suggest a seasonal use and not much else. Such was the availability of certain assets that BR could easily condone such lavish use. By July 1955 however time was up for the pair at Polmadie; No.40916 was withdrawn whilst No.41131 was transferred to Stranraer where in April of the following year it too was condemned. The Compounds were by then on their way out, BR having little use for them. *C.J.B. Sanderson (ARPT).*

The 35-ton engine hoist located at the south-west corner of the shed building with BR Standard Cl.3 No.77018 stabled beneath for convenience on 25th April 1965. The jib of the depot's breakdown crane can be seen on the right whilst another Standard looms on the left and mirrors somewhat the allocation of the period which was consisting almost half ex-LMS Standard types, and BR Standards. No.77018 was one of five 2-6-0s received new by Hurlford in 1954. *K. Gregory (ARPT).*

Standard Cl.3 No.77016 alongside the Stores, Blacksmiths, Joiners and Foreman's Office block on Sunday 17th May 1964 with resident Ivatt Cl.2 No.46451 behind. The five Cl.3s – Nos.77015 to 77019 – came new to Hurlford shed during July, August, and September 1954 from Swindon works, the last examples of the class although the original intention was to complete twenty-five of them with the final five allocated to the North Eastern Region but they were cancelled in September 1956 as common sense was slowly dawning amongst the BR hierarchy! All five of the Hurlford batch remained at the depot until withdrawal in 1966 and they were joined by sister No.77007 in August 1963 which was also condemned at 67B in November 1966. By the date of this image there was little work for these engines, diesel multiple units having taken over on those branches still open, and the freight work was mainly coal workings from the mines which were in the hands of Hughes/Fowler 'Crabs' and Stanier Cl.5s, and then diesel-electric Type 1s and Type 2s. Muirkirk could account for one of the 2-6-0s but even that place was losing its coal traffic. Hurlford depot was no longer required and in December 1966 the ninety-year old shed was closed, redundant and surplus. The remaining Cl.3s were the last of their kind in Scotland but by then everything was fast becoming 'the last of' so nothing was really noticed as it should have been. *A. Ives (ARPT).*

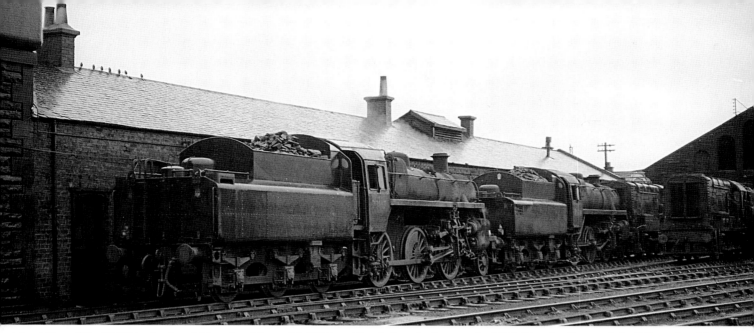

(above) **Two of the Cl.3 Standards rubbing shoulders with 350 h.p. diesel-electric shunters in 1964. Maurice Burns.** *(below)* **More shoulder rubbing at an earlier date when 2P No.40662 was still active; the 4-4-0 was withdrawn in September 1954.** *K.H. Cockerill (ARPT).*

(*above*) **Hurlford engine shed in all its unkempt glory on an unknown date in the 1960s with Stanier Cl.5s Nos.44727 and 44972 identified and anonymous 350 h.p. 0-6-0DE shunters representing the small occupancy.** (*below*) **Plenty of activity at the west side of the shed on that unknown date; although its motion has been stripped, No.44972 is in steam!** *Both Frank Coulton.*

MUIRKIRK

Being a sub of Hurlford, Muirkirk got all of its motive power supplied by 67B as witness 2P No.40688 outside the shed on Saturday 19th May 1956. These 4-4-0s took over from ex-Caley 3Ps on passenger turns to the likes of Lanark but Muirkirk only required half a dozen engines when BR took over, the majority being 0-6-0 tender engines of both CR and LMS vintages; the tender coupled to 4F No.44281 can be seen on the left of the picture. The 0-6-0 had been working local target 178 before retiring on shed. This building dated from 1879 – it replaced an earlier two-road shed – and was of typical G&SWR Galloway design, substantially constructed in stone. Now, some seventy-odd years later, subsidence, fire and general lack of maintenance found the structure in need of repair and or demolition. A compromise was decided whereby the northern half the shed nearest the main line was taken down and the remaining section repaired. The turntable was of 50ft diameter and was provided by Cowans Sheldon of Carlisle for the opening of the shed. It is interesting to see the remains of the doors which in this case were just that, remains! *F.W. Hampson (ARPT).*

The rebuilt shed in 1959 with two roads under cover. Outside 4F No.44198 and an unidentified ex-Caley 3F – both equally filthy – take in the afternoon sun. The CR had stabled engines here long before the Grouping and shortly after they became the main motive power as the 'Sou-Western classes were decimated by the LMS. *K.H. Cockerill (ARPT).*

Further detail from 23rd September 1961; the place had been adapted to accept the new upper gable screen, and the new north wall. The people who provided a new door and window in the office section did not bother employing the skills of a stonemason; perhaps the job was given to a private contractor who was fed the line that the shed would not be open much longer! Anyway modellers take note of those discrepancies within the stonework; at least those pieces of rotten timber masquerading as doors in the illustration on page 33 have been removed. Muirkirk engine shed closed in October 1964. *Howard Forster.*

Ayr shed yard, south end, April 1966 with a bias towards Stanier products hogging the premises. On the left is the extension built in 1959 along with a similar structure at the north end of the shed. Diesel locomotives had already started to infiltrate the depot here – diesel shunters had been allocated since 1952 – and that lightweight extension was purely for their use with a division straight down the inside of the shed between Nos.3 and 4 roads. *(D.R. Dunn collection)*.

The south end of the engine shed yard circa June 1954 as seen from the footbridge which straddled the Ayr to Newton line, besides connecting the shed yard with Viewfield Road. The only two engines identified are both from Kingmoor – 4F No.44189 and 'Crab' No.42802 – whilst everything else is a mixture of residents and visitors. *K.H. Cockerill (ARPT)*.

Another look from the footbridge but now in April 1966! *(D.R. Dunn collection).*

(opposite, top) **The subject of this undated image is the Fowler tender which has been uncoupled from its engine for reasons unknown but nevertheless the photograph allows us to see detail which is otherwise hidden. However, what caught this compilers' eye was the 67C shed plate on the grounded snowplough on the right of the image. The Scottish Region did allocate ploughs of various sizes to depots but to see that a shed plate had been fitted and where was news. The Cl.4 is No.76098 whilst the wheelset appears to want another axle-box and associated springing. Frank Coulton. *(opposite)* Getting prepared for another bad spell! Cl.5 No.45497 wears**
38 **the aforementioned snow plough on 1st September 1963. The driver of the diesel railcar looks on in awe!** *C.J.B. Sanderson (ARPT).*

2P No.40664 at the north end of the shed yard on 16th September 1959; the north end extension to roads 1, 2, and 3 is rapidly taking shape. The building was extended initially to accommodate diesel multiple units which would be running an Inter-City service to Glasgow. The clock was ticking! *C.J.B. Sanderson (ARPT).*

None of the stone-built grandeur of Galloway's style of engine shed here at Ardrossan; this simple brick-built utilitarian design reflects the 1894 building date when efficiency more than anything else was what mattered to the G&SWR. The four-road shed was double-ended with wide doorways topped with rolled steel joists. The circular openings in each gable were the only deviation from the straight lines otherwise employed in the building. Our 11th August 1962 image recorded at the south end of the shed shows Stanier Cl.5 No.45251 complete with 67D shed plate alongside BR Std. 5 No.73122 from Corkerhill; arriving new along with sisters Nos.73121, 73123, and 73124, the four Standards spent the whole of their short lives working from 67A. The Stanier engine having had a longer existence also had a more interesting allocation history having started work at Tebay in September 1936 and then to Patricroft in June 1939. It transferred to the LMS Northern Division in Scotland during October 1942 with the magnet of Perth applying full power. A brief but nevertheless two years and four months spell at Polmadie saw its first incursion to Glasgow before returning to Perth. Transferred in July 1947 to Corkerhill, the 4-6-0 remained at what was to become 67A for some twelve years. Finally, in October 1959 it was sent to Ardrossan to join the growing steam allocation at the Ayrshire depot – unusually the shed had undergone a 20% rise in the numbers of locomotives allocated compared with a decade previously. It was withdrawn in December 1963, one year and three months before the closure of Ardrossan to steam locomotives. *C.J.B. Sanderson (ARPT).*

Prior to its working off shed to take up an unknown duty, 3F No.17579 gets fully oiled by its driver during the late afternoon of Friday 20th May 1949 at the north end of the shed. The McIntosh 0-6-0 had spent most of the LMS era in Ayrshire being initially shedded at Ayr and then Ardrossan from sometime during WWII. Note that the engine was fitted with a vacuum ejector and steam heating making it very versatile. Although it transferred to Corkerhill from June 1952, No.57579 was back at Ardrossan in September 1957. Withdrawal took place in November 1961 and the 3F was later sold for scrap. *K.H. Cockerill (ARPT).*

Time to illustrate the 2-8-0 version of the WD Austerity locomotives which plied their way around most of Scotland from the post-war years until the end of steam on the Region; (above) No.90505 here by the coal stage at Ardrossan is not perhaps such a good example because it was on the date of this photograph – 11th August 1962 – already withdrawn! Having arrived at Ardrossan on 28th January 1961 from Ayr, the 2-8-0 went about its business until 11th June 1962 when it became one of the early casualties on the Scottish Region. 67D acquired five of them – 90198, 90319, 90463, 90505, and 90549 – between late January 1961 and April 1962. Only two of those were withdrawn at the shed, the others moving elsewhere in 1962. Besides 90505 we present sister 90463 (below) which had yet to be withdrawn but would become 'the other one' on 30th November 1963. Note that 90505 had not acquired a boiler with the BR Standard clack valves whereas 90463 had; a Scottish flair it seems. *Both C.J.B. Sanderson (ARPT).*

68B DUMFRIES

Dumfries engine shed as seen from the vantage point of the Annan Road bridge; the date is 13th August 1960 and the Saturday afternoon sun highlights a couple of 'Crabs' Kingmoor's No.42913 and resident No.42918. Other identified locomotives include recently transferred in 3F 0-6-0T No.56302 and another 3F, long-term resident 0-6-0 No.57621. By now the six-road dead-end, 1878-built shed had lost its ornate upper gable screens which included arched and glazed window openings which allowed – initially – a good amount of daylight to penetrate the interior of the shed but smoke and grime, not to mention the lack of window cleaners in the area, soon rendered the windows useless. No doubt roof glazing then became necessary to counter the cave-like darkness. However, for some reason the original gables at the other end of the building survived to closure; this new screen was provided just before WWII with the western section being completed by the summer of 1937 before the eastern side screen was taken down and rebuilt. Considering some twenty-odd years had passed since the work was done, the brickwork is still reasonably clean. *R.H. Leslie.*

The view to the south-east from the western end of Annan Road bridge with the 60ft turntable located on the Up side of the main line and the coaling stage in the distance, and even further detached from the shed. The date is 8th April 1961, a Saturday, and our interest here is the group of 'dead' locomotives awaiting further orders. The gathering of seven consists of – in numerical order – Nos.40152, 40577, 40614, 54492, 55232, 57349, and 57623. Although none of the engines had been withdrawn to date, their fates at this stage had already been decided as follows: 40152 withdrawn January 1962; having started work at Macclesfield in September 1937, the Class 3 tank moved north to Dalry Road at the outbreak of WWII and spent the rest of its life at former LMS sheds in Scotland transferring to Dumfries from Dawsholm in May 1960. 2P No.40577 had spent the whole of its BR career at Dumfries and the later part of its LMS existence; withdrawal of the 4-4-0 took place just three months after this image was recorded. Sister 40614 followed a similar career path and it was withdrawn in October 1961. Ex-CR 3P No.54492 was an orphan from Stranraer which was conveniently deposited here awaiting withdrawal in December 1961; it never went back to the coast. No.55232 came to Dumfries from Beattock in the summer of 1958 having tired of the hills and the incessant thrashing of banking duties; its withdrawal took place in September 1961. Next are the two 0-6-0s; 2F No.57349 was another Dumfries regular which had been at the shed since early LMS days and which was about to succumb during the following July. No.57623 arrived at Dumfries from Dalry Road during WWII and remained until the end which came for the 3F in December 1961. It is of interest to note that all the tenders and bunkers have been emptied of coal and muck appertaining to be coal. *R.H. Leslie.*

No.40614 before it was dumped by the Annan Road bridge. The date is 6th June 1960, a Saturday, and the 2P 4-4-0 has been prepared for storage and even the shed plate has been removed! This is the siding on the east side of the shed where locomotives normally destined for main works would be stored prior to departure. *C.J.B. Sanderson (ARPT).*

Staying at the side of the shed on that 6ᵗʰ day of June 1960, we find another candidate for the Annan Road bridge dump – 2F No.57349. Revealing detail not normally on show, the 0-6-0 has both tender filler caps open but other items are missing such as the spectacle plates which would indicate that although the locomotive has yet to be withdrawn, its chances of working again were zero rated. Note that the pair are coupled together ready for the shunt which will take them onto those sidings on the Down side of the main line where they remained coupled until called to the scrapyard. *C.J.B. Sanderson (ARPT).*

Stabled in a siding on the north side of the Annan Road bridge on that first Saturday in June 1960, was 2F No.57378 another Dumfries engine of long-standing which was one of ten ex-Caley 0-6-0s allocated to the shed at this time. Just ten years beforehand the shed boasted sixteen such locomotives amongst its thirty-eight strong allocation but even that number was down from the twenty-one handed over by the LMS on the last day of 1947 (this engine being amongst them). The 2F had transferred to Dumfries from Motherwell before WWII and remained at the depot until withdrawn in September 1962. Dominating the background here is the aforementioned road bridge from where excellent views of the shed yard, and the main line could be got at any time. *C.J.B. Sanderson (ARPT).*

Looking onto the siding from the elevated position of the road bridge parapet on Sunday 30th June 1963 reveals 3F No.57600 giving the photographer a rather smoky greeting whilst simmering and awaiting business. Although this 0-6-0 was not one of the chosen few, some seventeen members of the original seventy-nine McIntosh '812' class were fitted with Westinghouse pumps and screw couplings for working passenger trains – Nos.812-828 – but the LMS took off the pumps and the blue Caledonian livery was changed to black like the rest of the class. The first engine to be withdrawn went in 1946 and two more were taken out of service by the LMS shortly before they were to become BR property but it took twenty-five years for BR to completely eliminate the class. However, one of their kind, from the original mixed traffic engines – No.57566 (CR – 828) – survives in preservation. *John Boyes (ARPT).*

We don't see too many views with engines under the hoist and or having a wheelset missing but this image from 19th July 1959 is satisfyingly complete. The fact that it is a Sunday resolves the closed workshop doors issue not to mention the hoist control cabin door being closed too – yes the original hand chain-powered mechanism was long ago replaced by an electric motor which easily lifted the front-end of any 0-6-0. Resident 3F No.57600 has also been separated from its tender, an operation necessary if drawbars are not to be bent! That repairs such as this were able to be carried out at Dumfries enabled the shed to be virtually self-contained and less reliant on the main shed in the group which was Kingmoor up to July 1962 when the 68B shed code was changed to 67E under Corkerhill. Located as it was at the southern end of the former Glasgow & South Western Railway network, and furthest perhaps from Kilmarnock works, the shed was bound to have facilities above average. No.57600 had been allocated to Dumfries since WWII and had come from Girvan where it had replaced the unwanted ex-G&SWR motive power. It was withdrawn at Dumfries in November 1963 and later sold to a private scrapping enterprise in Troon. *F.W. Hampson (ARPT)*.

Peppercorn A1 No.60154 BON ACCORD shares the same road with one of Kingmoor's Stanier Cl.5 – No.45013 – at a quiet Dumfries shed on 7th June 1965. The shed had rarely been this empty in all its eighty-odd years since becoming operational. The line to Stranraer had just closed and it was that route plus the branches thereon which gave Dumfries much of its work. Peppercorn A1s were quite a rarity around these parts and No.60154 had worked in from Leeds and appears serviced and ready to head back home where, some four months hence, it was condemned and sold for scrap. Just behind the smoke generated by the A1 is BR Standard Cl.4 No.76074 a recent – October 1964 – acquisition from Dawsholm and one which would outlive the shed here when it transferred to Ayr in March 1966. *John Boyes (ARPT).*

68C STRANRAER

The motive power depot here consisted essentially three different and distinct building which were the remnants of the original residents which made up the Portpatrick & Wigtownshire Joint Railway – the Caledonian Railway, and the Glasgow & South Western Railway – which existed from 1885 and which had been borne from earlier beginnings from the 1860s. Essentially the three sheds were from north to south: The Caley shed of two roads and visible on the right here with its closed doors and no longer in use for locomotive purposes by the June 1964 exposure of this image. The tall two-road shed was the old workshops, complete with 30-ton hoist, and which had been given over to day-to-day servicing as a running shed by this time; the original doorways were much narrower and arched, this modification was carried out by BR. The next shed was the one-road Girvan shed which was connected to the two-road Joint shed; both of these buildings had been heavily rebuilt by BR. This image shows the usual locomotive types working from Stranraer at this period with Stanier Cl.5 No.45470 ready for its next job; this engine transferred to Stranraer in October 1962 from Ardrossan having arrived on G&SWR metals at Corkerhill in April 1962 from a six-month stint at Inverness. The '5' had spent twenty-one years at Perth up to November 1961 but a couple of years at 67F saw it withdrawn in September 1964, just weeks after this scene was recorded. In the next bay is BR Standard Cl.2 No.78016 which with sister No.78026 came from Dumfries in February 1964 in exchange for a pair of Ivatt Cl.2s. No.78016 lasted the course at Stranraer and was withdrawn in August 1966 whereas No.78026 had already moved on to Corkerhill during November 1964. *J.W. Armstrong (ARPT)*.

A couple of former Caley old-timers stable on one of the roads extending north-westwards at the rear of the 'Joint' shed on Thursday 1st May 1958. The depot was coded 68C at this time and 2F No.57445 is wearing one such plate. A long term resident in BR terms, the 0-6-0 was one of the twelve-strong allocation of locomotives which saw the transition from LMS to BR ownership. Having spent much of the early LMS period at Polmadie, No.17445 was sent to Stranraer during WWII. Behind, 3P No.54508 was a rare visitor from St Rollox Balornock (65B). The ex-LMS 2P, No.40611, was stabled on the single road leading from the 'Girvan' shed and like the others is ready for its next duty. *C.J.B. Sanderson (ARPT)*.

Derelict, forlorn, condemned! Ex-CR 2F No.57375 had been withdrawn during November 1963 and the long serving Stranraer engine is now awaiting haulage to a scrap merchant in Troon. Stabled between the 'Joint' and 'Girvan' sheds, the 0-6-0 still wears the old BR emblem on its tender. *J.W. Armstrong (ARPT).*

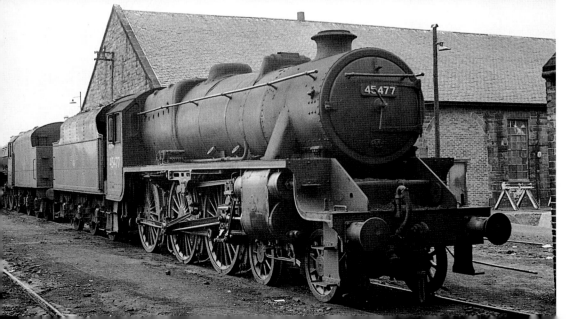

A resident and a visitor on Sunday 16th August 1964 – a smart looking No.44999 *(above)* which was a recent acquisition from Perth, and a not so smart No.45477 *(left)* from Edinburgh's Dalry Road looking more the part with another of the class behind on the western stub of the track behind the ex-CR shed. No.44999 remained at Stranraer until withdrawn in September 1966 and is stabled where 2F No.57375 spent its final months at 67F. *Both C.J.B. Sanderson (ARPT).*

68D BEATTOCK

Beattock's allocation at the end of summer 1935 consisted the following locomotives:

Ex-CR 2P 0-4-4T - 15161, 15163, 15164, 15181, 15217, 15237, 15238, 15239, and 15240.

These four-coupled tanks formed the sum of the banking engines employed on Beattock bank. Nos.15161 to 15217 were put into traffic between the turn-of-the-century and the beginning of World War One. The other four comprised the whole class of slightly modified ex-Caley banking engines built in 1922 and which were to last until 1961.

Ex-LNWR Railmotor 0-4-0T - 29988.

The railmotor was one of seven units listed by the LMS in the coaching stock series; its LMS number up to 1933 was 10698, its LNW number being 5505. No.29988 was the last of them and was not condemned until 1948 whereas all the others had been withdrawn by 1933. Its preserve was the Moffat branch where it worked until withdrawn.

In May 1944, in the lead up to D-Day, the allocation was little changed in type but had two extra engines thus:

Ex-CR 2P 04-4T - 15120, 15138, 15164, 15181, 15192, 15217, 15227, 15232, 15237, 15239, and 15262.

The two low number engines came from batches built in 1895 and 1898. No.15262 was one of the ten 1925 LMS built lot supplied by Nasmyth, Wilson.

Ex-LNWR Railmotor 0-4-0T - 29988 (having taken over from locomotive haulage of the 1 mile 71 chains long Moffat branch trains circa 1926, this vehicle became known as the 'Moffat Bus' or 'Puffer.').

On the last day of the LMS the allocation began to show radical changes as follows:

Ex-CR 0-4-4T - 15164, 15181, 15232, 15237, 15239.
Ex-CR 4-6-2T - 15350, 15351, 15352, 15353, 15354, 15356, 15359, 15360, 15361.
Ex-LNWR Railmotor 0-4-0T - 29988.

The entire surviving members of Pickersgill's CR 1917-built Pacific 'Wemyss Bay' tank engines bar one – No.15355 was still at Greenock – had been brought in to Beattock from Polmadie and Greenock to work their final years on banking duties in 1946, displaced by new Fairburn 2-6-4Ts. They were going out with a bang! Note that five of the four-coupled tanks had been retained to keep them company; that number would rise as the 4-6-2Ts were gradually withdrawn. No.15355 never joined the rest and was withdrawn at Ladyburn during that first month of Nationalisation.

Within a couple of years of BR taking over the 0-4-4Ts were back in force with nine on the books. But they would start to disappear from the banking jobs as new Fairburn 2-6-4Ts became available to take up banking duties. The 4-6-2Ts had all gone to the scrapyard by October 1953, displaced again by those 2-6-4Ts!

The north end of the engine shed on 29th March 1964 with Cl.4 tank No.42688 peeping from behind a Southern Region utility van, BR Standard Cl.4 No.76090 inside the shed, and ex-Caley 3F 0-6-0 No.57568 stored outside. The doors were fitted by the LMS and miraculously this set survived to the end of steam at Beattock. The shed consisted of two buildings the northern half dated from 1847 and was quite substantial with stone walls supported by buttresses between each window opening and on each corner. The southern half of the shed dated from 1857 and was somewhat narrower than the older building and had a more austere appearance with render covering the stone walls. *John Boyes (ARPT).*

Ex-CR 2P No.55234 basks in the early evening sun on 2nd May 1953 outside the north end of the shed. One of the BR additions to the allocation, this four-coupled tank remained at the shed until withdrawn in January 1963. It was sold to one of the private scrap yards. The gradient of the ten mile bank up to the summit averaged between 1 in 69 and 1 in 88, which was steep enough ordinarily but add 500-ton passenger trains and you can understand the requirement to have bankers. These four-coupled tanks and their predecessors managed the banking duties for over a hundred years and it was only towards the end of steam on BR that six-coupled locomotives took over. *C.J.B. Sanderson (ARPT).*

We always try to include one item of former passenger rolling stock which has been seconded by the relevant Running or Departmental organisations after withdrawal from passenger carrying duties but in this album we have surpassed ourselves hopefully with your approval. Remember these vehicles were all part of the motive power depot scene making them look either untidy or efficiently prepared. This example was a Caledonian Railway Brake and five-compartment composite from goodness knows when. It appears to have been abandoned by its last users and may well have been awaiting haulage to a place of scrap. The date of the image is 2nd May 1953 and yes there is some nice detail for any modellers of such items of stock. *C.J.B. Sanderson (ARPT).*

Another ex-CR 2P taking in the evening sun on that second day of May in 1953 was No.55187 which had started the decade at Oban shed but had gradually made its way south as though trying to escape the inevitable. It arrived at Beattock in September 1952 via a nine month stint in Forfar, and was fitted with that 68D shedplate – an artefact which nowadays must be quite rare – but look at the BRITISH RAILWAYS insignia which was applied with, perhaps, a view to inserting a BR emblem between the words. Also, look at the size of the figures and letters used; not quite St Rollox so was that last overhaul which saw the livery applied a Kilmarnock job? As things turned out the 0-4-4T never did get the BR emblem because after its December 1955 transfer to Corkerhill, it was withdrawn during the following February. This image is testimony that modelling BR steam locomotives alone can easily consist of a myriad of livery variations. *C.J.B. Sanderson (ARPT).*

Looking across the main line from the Up platform of Beattock station at No.42192 outside the south shed. This is the 1857 shed which was essentially a narrow extension of the 1847 shed. Note that only one opening was available at this end, an outbuilding had been erected where the original entrance, if ever there was one, would have been located. Steep slated pitched roofs were the norm around these parts to make sure that snow did not accumulate on what was basically the weakest part of a building. *J.W. Armstrong (ARPT).*

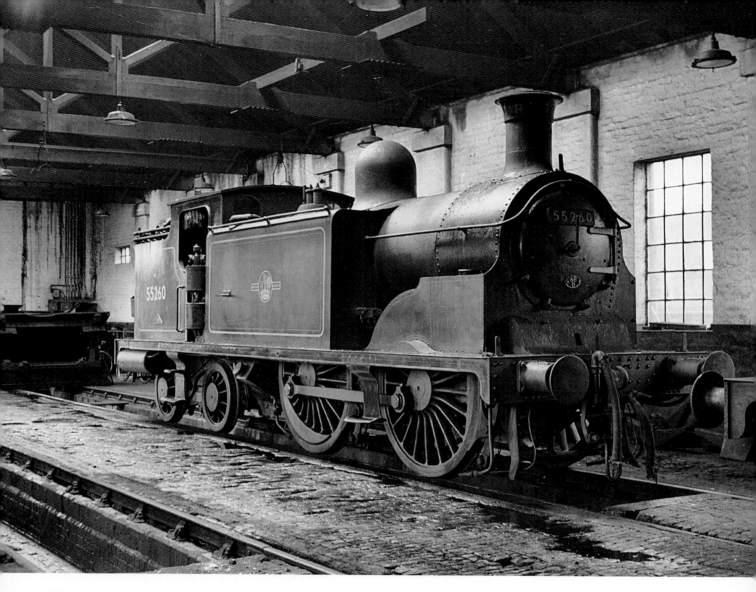

The interior of the southern end of the shed with Nasmyth, Wilson LMS enlarged-CR 2P 0-4-4T No.55260 stabled on 24th May 1958. This is the dead-end road on the west side of the shed, a convenient location for one of the depot's snowplough units. Electric lighting was provided from an early date in BR times and the conduits can been seen in the south-west corner competing with the roof leaks for wall space! All of the 1925-built four-coupled tanks worked from Beattock as one time or another, No.55260 was one of the latecomers; note the wrong-facing new BR crest applied during a recent shopping at St Rollox. *F.W. Hampson (ARPT).*

There is obviously a little bit of waiting taking place here in the siding where the on duty banking engines stabled awaiting business. It is a Saturday afternoon, 2nd May 1953 is the date, and the crew of Fairburn Class 4 tank No.42194 have retired to a more comfortable and accommodating location. It appears that oiling of the engine had been taking place and perhaps even a bit of cleaning may have been carried out but more than likely that overall 'finish' is courtesy of a recent visit to main works and a repaint. One of the BR Derby-built Cl.4 tanks, No.42192 spent the whole of its life in Scotland going initially to Corkerhill in February 1948 but headed south to Beattock in October 1952 from where it worked for the next twelve years until withdrawn in May 1964. *C.J.B. Sanderson (ARPT).*

Condenser-fitted ex-LMS Class 3 2-6-2T No.40021, stabled in the banking engine refuge siding on Monday 7th June 1954 just weeks before the six-coupled tank headed back to Kentish Town shed after a year on loan to Beattock. Why the Cl.3 was loaned to 68D in the first place is unknown but obviously a test of their prowess at banking was being tried. How it performed whilst resident is also unknown but it was certainly an unusual transfer for the Fowler tank and a long trial too. Entering traffic in November 1930 at Kentish Town shed the Cl.3MT spent the next sixteen years working the passenger services into London from the suburbs and swapping allegiance between Cricklewood and Kentish Town depots. Why this engine was chosen for the twelve-month stint in Scotland is unknown too but it went to Hellifield in March 1946 for a much longer residency returning to London in May 1952. So, what was a condenser fitted six-coupled tank doing in the wilds of Yorkshire for all that time? Perhaps it was one of those less than popular locomotives with the fitting staff which sheds' tended to try and get rid of but never quite manage to do so as they continue to return from whatever far-flung place its latest transfer took it? No.40021 ended its days at Kentish Town shed in September 1959 some twenty-nine years after it had first arrived! Note the lack of a shed plate which begs the question – did it ever get one of the 68D examples or had it recently been removed in anticipation of its imminent return to London? *C.J.B. Sanderson (ARPT).*

Before it became a semi-permanent fixture at this location, 3F No.57568 stables in the siding immediately behind the engine shed on the west side on an unknown date. This 0-6-0 arrived at Beattock in April 1956 from Dundee – it actually went initially, on paper, to Kingmoor shed in February but apparently never got that far south – the purpose of its transfer being unknown too but it remained at the depot long after it was withdrawn in November 1963. This view to the north shows the main line signal box and the bridge spanning the main line immediately north of the depot. *A. Dodgson (ARPT).*

'Wemyss Bay' tank No.55353 is coaled using the primitive but effective apparatus employed at Beattock for decades. Although undated, this image must have been recorded after 1949 when Beattock lost its LMS shed code 12F in favour of the new Scottish Region code 68D which can be seen nicely picked-out on the front of the Pacific tank along with the other temporary 'adornments' applied for an unknown event involving just the front-end of this engine. No.55353 was withdrawn in July 1951; Nos.55351 – February 1949; 55354 – September 1949; and 55356 – July 1950; had already gone beforehand. *S.C. Crook (ARPT)*.

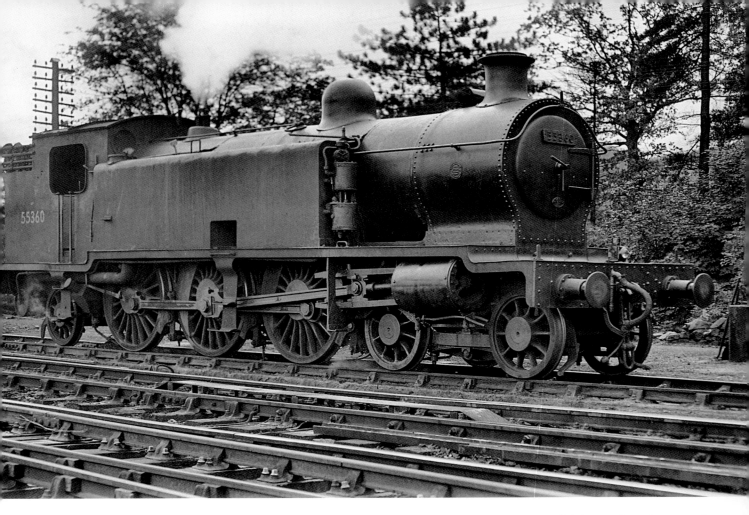

These Pacific tanks had been here before of course; three of them arrived when new but they didn't stay long because the superheater elements found it somewhat difficult to withstand the temperature extremities when banking and then idling at the bottom of the bank awaiting business. They were of course 'sorted-out' for their next residency at Beattock. This is No.55360 looking all business and purposeful on 24th September 1950. They were rated by BR at 4P which was the same as an LMS Compound or essentially a Stanier or Fairburn mixed-traffic tank. It was withdrawn in February 1952 leaving just four of the class working from the shed. *C.J.B. Sanderson (ARPT).*

To finish off our snapshot of the ex-CR Pacific tanks, we present the last of them, No.55359 which when withdrawn in October 1953 saw the class cease to exist. They had gone the course of what the accountants wanted with most of them putting thirty-odd years work in before being scrapped. The others allocated to Beattock which went before No.59 here were Nos.55350 in March 1952; 55352 also in March 1952; and 55361 in May 1952. Our subject was on shed on 25th May 1952 and note that a front numberplate has not been fitted although the bolts are there so has some souvenir hunter removed said plate? It would be nice to know if the big engine ever got a BR numberplate. *C.J.B. Sanderson (ARPT).*

The date is 26th May 1963, a Sunday, and two Ivatt period Derby-built tank engines – Nos.42215 and 42205 – are stored in a siding just south of the running shed on the Down side. The pair were actually withdrawn having been condemned during the previous December. Both of the six-coupled tanks were just seventeen years old when retired but it was the age of 'get rid of steam at all costs' so their fates were sealed. Although ending up at Beattock shed, the engines had different starts to their short careers with No.42205 going initially to the LMS Central Division shed at Huddersfield in November 1945; four months later it was transferred to Wigan Central and by June 1946 was resident at Accrington. Once the summer timetable was completed, No.2205 – as it was then – was transferred to Polmadie where it joined many others of its type. Moving away from Glasgow via Motherwell, Perth and then Blair Atholl where it proved itself on banking duties, it finally arrived at Beattock in May 1954. No.42215 on the other hand was sent new to Polmadie in December 1945 along with a number of classmates. In March 1946 she was amongst a party of five – 2213 to 2217 – sent to Kyle of Lochalsh of all places where they worked until the end of that year's summer timetable and by the end of September 1946 they were back at Polmadie. Having had a taste of fresh air on the west coast No.42215 and two sisters – 42213 and 42214 – took up residence at Beattock in March 1952 for – in No.42215's case – ten years of relentless banking of some of BR's heaviest passenger trains. The eagle-eyed amongst you will note that the nearest engine had been fitted with ATC whereas No.42205 had not. Also note that both engines had received various tank repairs where rivets rather than welding had been used to affix patches; 42215 has a least half a dozen patches of different sizes. Where did the pair eventually end up? Motherwell Machinery & Scrap purchased them for the going rate and they were hauled north, complete with chimney caps, not long after this image was recorded. *C.J.B. Sanderson (ARPT)*.

BR Cl.4 No.76090 came to Beattock in July 1962 from Motherwell. This was its final shed and it was withdrawn in December 1966, not quite the end for steam but not too far off; sisters 76094 and 76098 had the honour, distinction, of performing those last duties. This image is undated but the front end is smart enough – methinks a trip to Cowlairs had recently taken place – with picked-out number and shed plates and that all important Cowlairs touch of painting the name of the home shed on the bufferbeam. By now Beattock was 66D under the care of Polmadie. *Chris Campbell.*

A derelict No.57568 at the rear of the shed in April 1964! This image allows us to see both buildings and their relationship with each other. The shed survived steam banking, and even provided shelter for the diesels used for banking chores. However, by 1978 it had been largely left unused and was demolished bringing to an end over one-hundred and thirty years of banking on one of the toughest main-line inclines in Britain. *C.J.B. Sanderson (ARPT).*

Beattock's reason for existence! Two BR Standards – Cl.4 No.80111 and Cl.4 No.76090 wait in the siding alongside Beattock South signal box on a murky Monday 29th August 1966. We are now into the last year when steam locomotives were used for banking northbound trains up the bank here. By now BR Standards have taken over most of the duties but their time is running out and diesel locomotives would soon be taking up the role for the next decade before the introduction of electric traction on this main line. No.80111 – on loan from Polmadie – is taking on water from the column provided specifically for the banking engines which had been stabled in this siding for more than a century. The last steam locomotives working the bank here were Cl.4s Nos.76094 and 76098 which were fairly latecomers to Beattock and ended up being withdrawn in May 1967 when replaced by Clayton Type 1 diesel locomotives. The water column nearest the camera has probably not been used for some time and it would most probably never be used again as the rush to rid the region of steam traction became more apparent as each month of 1966 passed. BR Cl.4 tank engines allocated here arrived from various sheds but mainly from Polmadie as follows: 80001 arrived May 1962 ex 66A to 66A May 1964; 80002 ditto; 80004 ex 61A June 1961 to 65A December 1962; 80005 ex 67C March 1965 to 66A November 1965; 80006 ex 66A June 1961 to 66A August 1961; 80091 ex 67B April 1966 to withdrawal 29th November 1966; 80111 ditto; 80117 ex 67E November 1965 to 66A November 1965. There were also those on loan from Polmadie such as No.80111. *John Boyes (ARPT).*